VIKING AND
THE MARS LANDING

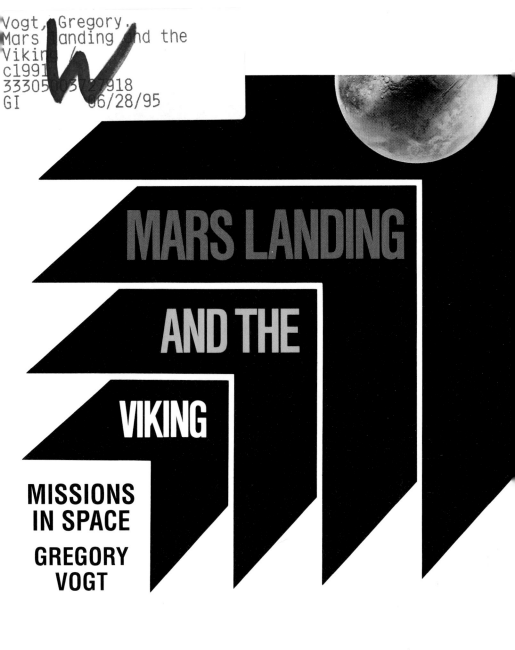

MARS LANDING

AND THE

VIKING

MISSIONS
IN SPACE
GREGORY
VOGT

THE MILLBROOK
PRESS

BROOKFIELD,
CONNECTICUT

Cover photograph courtesy of NASA

Photographs courtesy of NASA: pp. 3, 10, 28, 39, 44, 47, 48, 51, 52, 54, 55, 61, 67, 78–79, 84–85, 91, 92, 93, 94, 97, 100; The Bettmann Archive: pp. 16, 17, 22, 23, 24, 26, 34; NASA photo by the Lunar and Planetary Library, University of Arizona: p. 37; NASA, Jet Propulsion Laboratory: pp. 52, 66, 70, 80, 81, 87; Tass/Sovfoto: p. 99.

Library of Congress Cataloging-in-Publication Data

Vogt, Gregory.
Viking and the Mars Landing / by Gregory Vogt.
p.   :   col. ill.   ; (Missions in Space)
Includes bibliographical references (p.   )
Includes index (p.   )
Summary: Discusses the U.S. space program Viking and the mission to Mars.
1. Mars (Planet)—Juvenile literature.
2. Viking Mars Program—Juvenile literature.
3. Space flight to Mars—Juvenile literature.   629.4354
ISBN: 1-878841-32-7

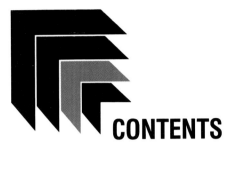

CONTENTS

It is with affection and respect that I dedicate this book to a dear and beautiful friend, Barbara G. Hollander, to tell her how much she is appreciated.

VIKING AND
THE MARS LANDING

# PREFACE

Across the vast reaches of interplanetary space the Red Planet Mars beckons to us. It is an alien world whose name inspires both interest and fear. During the most favorable times to observe the planet, when Earth and Mars are nearest to each other in their orbits, Mars appears blood-red against the coal-black night sky.

Of all the known planets, Mars is most like Earth in environment and composition. Humans have long speculated that Mars might harbor life forms, but if so, what sort? To answer this question and a host of others, various spacecraft have been sent to the Red Planet to ferret out its secrets. The most ambitious of these were the two *Viking* orbiters and landers that were sent to Mars in the middle 1970s. Their stunning success and the accomplishments of their forerunners have revealed much about the third nearest neighbor to Earth after the Moon and Venus. This is the story of the *Viking* mission, the events that led up to it, and what we know about Mars because of *Viking*.

CHAPTER ONE
THE MARTIANS
ARE COMING

Through the cold inky blackness of interplanetary space, a cold red world, the planet Mars, slowly orbits the Sun. Its atmosphere is thin and its oceans have receded to barely cover a third of its surface, leaving the land behind desert-dry. The slow change of seasons alternately gathers moisture into ice at the poles and then melts it to flood the equatorial regions. The harsh environment of this dying world has, by necessity, sharpened the intelligence of Martians living there to a level far surpassing that of the humans inhabiting its nearest planetary neighbor, the lush green and watery blue planet called Earth. As the end of Martian life nears, the Martians have only two paths they can choose: wither and die with the oceans or cross interplanetary space and claim Earth as a new home!

For a century, humans have considered Mars to be an Earthlike planet, one likely to sustain life. Telescopic observations of the surface have led to much conjecture, both scientific and fictional, on what Martian life forms might look like, should they exist, and how they might live. H. G. Wells, an Englishman born in 1866, wrote a wonderful science fiction story in 1898 about a Martian invasion of Earth. He called it *War of the Worlds*. The passage above is loosely adapted from it. However, the story begins:

No one would have believed in the last years of the nineteenth century that this world was being watched keenly and closely by intelligences greater than man's and yet as mortal as his own; that as men busied themselves about their various concerns they were scrutinized and studied, perhaps almost as narrowly as a man with a microscope might scrutinize the transient creatures that swarm and multiply in a drop of water. . . . Yet across the gulf of space . . . [Martians] regarded this earth with envious eyes, and slowly and surely drew their plans against us.

Wells's story is told through the voice of an English scholar. Earth astronomers, who detect strange things as their telescopes point toward the Red Planet, warn the world that something very unusual is happening. They observe flashes of light coming from the Martian surface. Soon it is learned that the flashes are the belching fire of a huge cannon blasting spacecraft toward Earth. The first spacecraft arrives several days later, streaking across the English sky. At first, it is believed to be a giant meteorite, but scientists arriving at the impact site soon realize that the blunt cylindrical vessel almost buried in sand is anything but a meteorite. Later, as curious crowds of people press in to get a look at the extraterrestrial visitor, the end cap of the craft begins unscrewing and drops into the side of the pit. A Martian slowly emerges. The story's narrator describes the creature to be about the size of a bear, with oily, funguslike skin that glistens like wet leather. The Martian has two large, dark-colored eyes and a V-shaped mouth that drips saliva. Its arms and legs are thin tentacles. It seems to the observer that the creature is having a difficult time adjusting to Earth's thicker atmosphere and stronger gravity.

A little later in the story, a small group of humans tries to communicate with the visitors, and that is when the real horror begins:

Beyond the pit [where the cylinder lay] the little wedge of people with the white flag at its apex . . . a little knot of small vertical black shapes upon the ground [silhouetted by a green glow from the pit]. As the green smoke arose, their faces flashed out pallid green and faded again as it vanished. Then slowly the hissing passed into a humming, into a long, loud droning noise. Slowly a humped shape rose out of the pit, and the ghost of a beam of light

seemed to flicker out from it. Forthwith flashes of actual flame, a bright glare leaping from one to another, sprang from the scattered group of men. It was as if some invisible jet impinged upon them and flashed into white flame. It was as if each man were suddenly and momentarily turned to fire.

The Martian attack had begun. The Martians, inside nearly indestructible three-legged walking machines and piloting flying machines, soon fanned across the countryside, destroying with

their heat rays and with poisonous black smoke any humans they could find and crushing hastily deployed artillery companies attempting to halt their advance. More cylinders landed, thrusting the whole world into war.

Eventually, the Martian attack came to an end, but not due to the efforts of the human defenders. Instead, the Martians were "slain by the putrefactive and disease bacteria [of Earth] against which their systems were unprepared . . . by the humblest things that God, in his wisdom, has put on this earth."

A host of other fiction writers created stories about Mars while scientists sought to learn the true nature of the Red Planet. Joining Wells, for example, was Edgar Rice Burroughs, the creator of the Tarzan stories. Burroughs writes about John Carter, a Virginian who is transported to Mars and discovers a fantastic world populated by warring races of red, green, white, black, and yellow people and hideous, flesh-eating monsters. Mars itself is a world of dusty plains, lush valleys, caves, subterranean seas, and polar ice barriers.

Certainly the most bizarre episode to occur in relation to Mars involved a radio show. And it was not the story that was bizarre—it was the reaction of the listeners.

The radio show aired at 8:00 P.M. Eastern Standard Time, on October 30, 1938—Halloween eve. It was a dramatization of *War of the Worlds* presented by the Mercury Theater on the Columbia Broadcasting System. The actor and director Orson Welles and a small group of actors and sound-effects personnel created a fictional newscast based on the H. G. Wells story, but instead of landing in England, the first Martian cylinder was reported seen on a farm in Grovers Mill, New Jersey.

The acting and sound effects were wonderful. Actors impersonating news reporters described horrible scenes of heat rays torching the countryside, Martian walking machines, and poisonous black smoke. With terror and despair in their voices they told listeners of how U. S. military forces were helpless to prevent the destruction or even save their own lives. To heighten the drama, one on-the-scene reporter's words were cut off in midsentence, giving the impression that the reporter had been killed by a heat ray.

Many of the estimated 7 million people listening to the radio drama greatly enjoyed the unfolding story. However, many other listeners tuned in late and did not hear the announcement that the program was a radio play. A large number of those listeners believed that the program was a real newscast and Martians were actually destroying the Earth! Panic was widespread. Across the country people abandoned their homes to run aimlessly through the streets, seek shelter in churches, or drive into the countryside to hide out in the hills. Still others began sealing the cracks around their windows to keep out the "black smoke." A few even seriously prepared to commit suicide rather than let the Martians get them!

One explanation for the panic was that, at that time, the world was on the verge of another major war, and the possibility of an invasion was a fact of life. Why not an invasion from Mars? But a bigger reason was that over the years several prominent scientists had publicly expressed their belief that life on Mars, even intelligent life, was a distinct possibility.

THE GREAT MARTIAN CANAL CONTROVERSY

Ancient observers of heavenly bodies thought they could predict the course of events according to what they thought were the motions of the stars in the night sky. Like the Sun and the Moon, the stars were believed to rise and set each day. Unknown to these observers, however, was that stellar motions were only apparent. The real cause of the motion was the rotation of the Earth. But some stellar objects did move. Mars, they discovered, was one of a small number of these objects that slowly wandered among the stars. It was called a *planet,* a word originally derived from the Greek word *planetes,* meaning "wanderers."

Though early observations of the planets were used mainly for astrology or fortunetelling, they did establish that these objects moved independently among the stars. Because of those movements, ancient observers attributed godlike properties to the planets. Mars was named after the Roman god of war.

Much later, toward the end of the sixteenth century, very precise observations of the movements of Mars over many years were made by a Danish astronomer named Tycho Brahe. The data Brahe collected helped another astronomer in the early seventeenth century, a German named Johannes Kepler, prove that planets travel in elliptical, or egg-shaped, orbits around the Sun. More than sixty years earlier, a Polish church official named Nicolaus Copernicus had published a book stating that all the planets, including the Earth, orbited the Sun. His work aroused much controversy, because the powerful Roman Catholic Church taught that the Earth, not the Sun, was at the center of the universe. The Church threatened to punish with imprisonment or even death anyone who publicly supported Copernicus's theory. Brahe's Mars observations and Kepler's interpretation of them did just that. Although of little practical significance at the time, knowing the precise movements of Mars would one day be of extreme importance, when spacefaring nations would begin sending robot spacecraft to the Red Planet.

In the early seventeenth century, Italian astronomer Galileo Galilei turned the newly invented astronomical telescope toward the heavens. One of his interests was Mars, and through a telescope that magnified the planet only thirty-two times, Galileo observed that Mars appeared as a round disk, like the Moon. In 1659 another astronomer, Christian Huygens, made sketches of Mars that revealed some dark shadows on the surface of the planet. For the next two hundred years, as better telescopes were constructed, scientific information about Mars increased. The

Facing page: Danish astronomer Tycho Brahe (1546–1601) in his observatory. *Right:* The German astronomer Johannes Kepler (1571–1630). Polish astronomer Nicolaus Copernicus (1473–1543) is below.

Christian Huygens (1629–1695), Dutch mathematician, physicist, and astronomer.

planet's rotation (day) was deduced to be nearly twenty-four hours, and whitish polar caps and faint dusty markings were observed. By the 1800s, scientists concluded that Mars was very similar to Earth except that the land was redder. Like Earth, Mars probably had oceans, clouds, and snow.

The scientific belief that Mars might be teeming with life started with a misunderstanding. In 1877, Giovanni Virginio Schiaparelli, director of the Brera Observatory in Milan, Italy, began some twenty years of intensive study of Mars. He meticulously sketched maps of the surface markings he saw on the planet through his telescope. Some of the markings appeared to be linear, or running in straight lines, and he called them *canali,* an Italian word that means "channels." Schiaparelli assumed these features to be waterways, and he named some of them after important rivers on Earth. As the years passed, Schiaparelli's maps of Mars became more detailed and intricate. Eventually, he identified what he thought were 113 *canali.*

Schiaparelli's first public mention of his discovery of the channels appeared in a report he wrote in 1878 entitled "Astronomical and Physical Observations of the Axis and Rotation and on the Topography of the Planet Mars." In part because it made Mars seem so much like Earth, Schiaparelli's paper caused much excitement. Most people heard of the paper through news reports that summarized its findings. Through carelessness, reporters mistranslated *canali* into

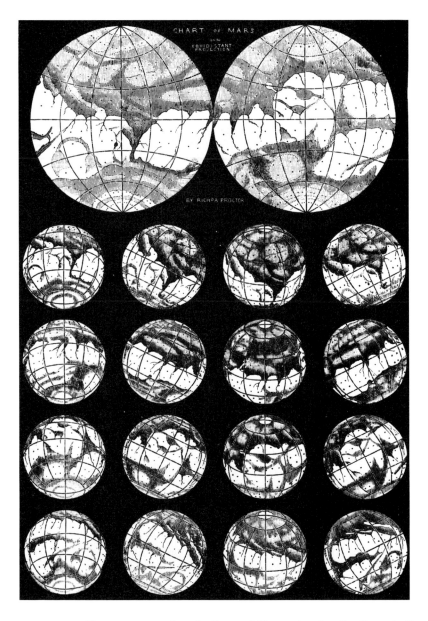

These maps and projections of Mars, showing the "canals,"
were made from drawings by Schiaparelli and others.

the English word "canals." Canals on Earth are constructed by human beings, not natural forces, and so the use of the word touched off widespread speculation that the Martian "canals" might have been constructed by intelligent beings—Martians.

Two American astronomers, William H. Pickering and Percival Lowell, added new observations to the rapidly growing body of knowledge about Mars. Pickering noticed dark spots at the junctions of many intersecting canals. He called them "lakes." Percival Lowell founded the Lowell Observatory in Flagstaff, Arizona, principally to study Mars. He saw the lakes as well but called them "oases." Eventually, he counted two hundred oases and increased Schiaparelli's canal count to over five hundred.

Lowell did much to stir the public's imagination by asserting that the canals were not the result of natural processes on Mars but constructed by "intelligent creatures, alike to us in spirit, though not in form." He wrote three books about Mars and pictured it as a dying planet whose civilization was desperately trying to transport water from the polar ice caps to the temperate zones to maintain life there. It was about this time that H. G. Wells and others began writing fantastic fictional accounts of Martian life. Even Schiaparelli got caught up in the intelligent-life-on-Mars fad. In 1897, he wrote that the "arrangement [of the canals] presents an

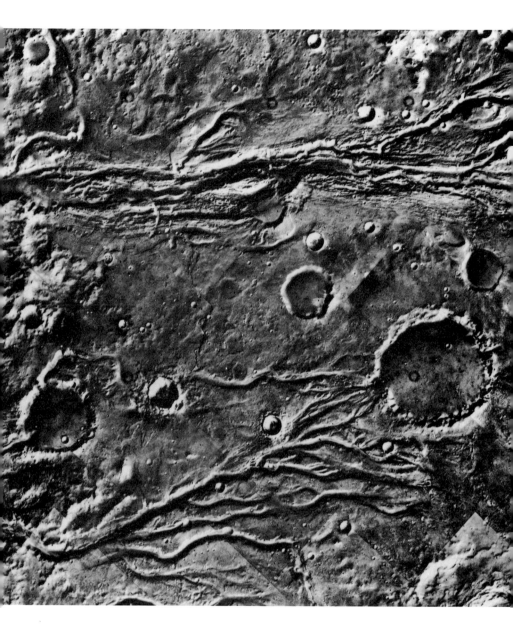

Long, branching channels, possibly carved
by flowing water, can be seen clearly in this
photograph of the Martian surface.

indescribable simplicity and symmetry which cannot be the work of chance.''

Not every astronomer who looked at Mars saw the canals. Drawings by the ones who did varied widely in shape and their arrangements. Some astronomers began to think that the canals did not exist at all. Chance alignments of shadowy features on the planet, they surmised, plus poor telescopes and less than ideal observing conditions combined to make overly eager observers see things that weren't really there. Naturally, a controversy erupted between those who were sure the canals existed and those who were sure they didn't.

It was well into the twentieth century before the controversy was finally settled. In the 1960s and early 1970s, the United States began sending spacecraft to Mars. None of the pictures of the planet radioed back to Earth showed any signs of the canals, and it was finally concluded that the canals were just shadows that appeared linear in the minds of imaginative observers.

However, one discovery about Mars made by the early spacecraft missions was the cause of some excitement. Many areas of the planet's surface were laced with channels. Though much too small to have been seen by Schiaparelli through his telescope, real channels—not canals—did exist on the planet. If the channels had been cut by running water, as seemed likely, it meant that there was a strong possibility that Mars could support at least simple Earth-type life forms. Could it be that there were Martians after all?

CHAPTER TWO
THE PLANET
MARS

Mars is the fourth planet outward from the Sun and together with Earth, Venus, and Mercury forms a relatively tight grouping called the *inner planets*. The fifth planet out is Jupiter, but Jupiter is more than three times farther from the Sun than Mars is. Jupiter and the more distant planets of our Solar System are called the *outer planets*.

As Johannes Kepler discovered in the early seventeenth century, the orbit of Mars is in the shape of an ellipse. The best way to understand an ellipse is to draw one. All you need is a piece of cardboard, a sheet of paper, two pins, a loop of string, and a pencil. Place the paper on the cardboard and stick one pin into the center. Next, tie a loop of string to form a circle about three inches in diameter. Place the loop over the pin and the point of the pencil inside the loop. Now pull the pencil point away from the pin as far as the string will allow and draw a shape completely around the pin. The shape drawn is a circle. Next, place a second pin into the paper about two inches from the first. Loop the string around both pins and again draw a shape. This shape is an ellipse. By moving the pins farther apart, the ellipse becomes flatter, and by moving them closer together, the ellipse becomes more like a circle.

Kepler discovered not only that all planets move in elliptical orbits but that the Sun is located at one of the two "pinpoints" that define each planetary orbit's elliptical shape. This means that all planets are closer to the Sun during part of their revolution than at other times. Earth has an elliptical orbit that is nearly circular in shape. The difference between its closest point to the Sun and its farthest is about one million miles. Mars's orbit is much more elliptical. Its difference is about 26 million miles.

At an average distance from the Sun of 142 million miles, Mars takes 687 Earth days to complete one revolution. It moves in its orbit at a rate of 15 miles per second. However, this is an average rate. Another of Kepler's discoveries was that the speed a planet travels depends upon its distance from the Sun. In an orbit like that of Mars, the planet will slow down as it moves away from the Sun and speed up as it nears the Sun. The situation is like tossing a ball in the air. The ball slows down as it flies upward and away from Earth and then speeds up again as Earth's gravity brings it back down. Like Earth,

Mars has seasons, and because of its changing orbital speed, spring in the Martian northern hemisphere lasts 52 days longer than fall.

Mars is smaller than Earth. Its diameter is 4,220 miles, and its mass is just over one-tenth that of the Earth's. Scientists speculate that the interior of Mars must be mostly rock, with possibly a small core of iron and sulfur. Averaging together the heavy materials in the planet's center with lighter surface rock gives the planet a density of 3.9. Density is how heavy something is in comparison to an equal volume of water. Mars is 3.9 times denser than water. Knowing these factors, scientists have calculated the planet's surface gravity to be 0.38 that of Earth's. In other words, a 100-pound person on Earth would weigh just 38 pounds on Mars!

The way scientists came up with these numbers is somewhat complicated. Much of what we know today about the physical properties of planets is based on the work of the great English scientist Sir Isaac Newton (1642–1727). Newton figured out a way to measure the force of gravity between two objects. Using this discovery, astronomers were able to work out the gravitational pull every planet has on every other planet. Since the pull of gravity diminishes with distance, they also had to know where every planet was at the time they made their calculations. Knowing this, they could calculate how big each planet was from how big it appeared in their telescopes. Next, they could estimate each planet's mass, density, and so on.

Isaac Newton (1642–1727) analyzing
a ray of light.

As we learned earlier, the telescope did much to expand our knowledge about the Red Planet. Unfortunately, telescopes are quite limited in what they can do, because of the atmosphere that surrounds the Earth. This atmosphere filters out some of the visible and invisible forms of light bombarding Earth from space. Atmospheric currents also cause light waves to shimmer, and this makes high-power telescope observations somewhat fuzzy. Finally, when we attempt to look at the surface of Mars, the Martian atmosphere can also interfere. Because it is smaller than Earth and has a much smaller gravitational pull at its surface, Mars is not able to retain much of an atmosphere. The air there is only about 1/150 the density of Earth's. In other words, the air at the surface has about the same pressure as you would expect to find on Earth at an elevation three to four times higher than that at which commercial jet planes fly. However this air, though very thin, is rich in carbon dioxide gas, and so still has distorting effects similar to Earth's air. Winds at the surface can also stir up giant dust storms that obscure the view for months at a time.

At best, when Mars and Earth are closest to each other in their respective orbits and when there are no Martian dust storms, the view of the planet seen through the largest Earth-based telescopes is still fuzzy. What is seen are shadowy-looking features in the equatorial region that seem to change from time to time and white polar caps that enlarge and shrink with Martian winters and summers. Though appearing fuzzy, those features have still permitted astronomers to calculate the length of a day on the planet. While watching the planet rotate, they see a distinctive marking that crosses the middle point of the planet and disappears on one side. The time of the middle crossing will be noted. When that same feature reappears on the other side of the planet and Mars's rotation brings it back to the middle, the time is again noted. The difference between the two times is the planet's rotation rate. In this manner it was learned that Mars has a rotation rate of 24 hours and 37 minutes.

Being farther from the Sun than the Earth is, the surface of Mars receives less sunlight. Light spreads out as it travels from its source, and in so doing its intensity is reduced. To see this for yourself, light a candle in a darkened room, hold it near one of the walls, then move it away. The diminishing of the light's intensity is governed by a scientific principle called the *inverse square law*. This simply means that if you double the distance from the candle to the wall, the light will only be one-fourth as intense. If you triple the distance or quadruple it, the light will be, respectively, only one-ninth or one-sixteenth as intense. The same is true of the intensity of sunlight on planets. Mars is about half again as far from the Sun as the Earth is. Because of this, the intensity of sunlight at its surface is slightly less than half of that on Earth.

With less sunlight reaching the surface of Mars, one would expect the planet to be colder than Earth, and this is true. But there is more to sur-

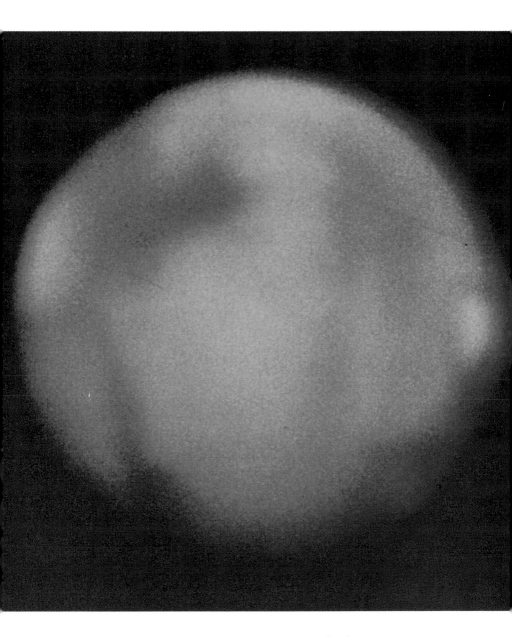

Even sophisticated telescopes on Earth cannot
reveal much detail on Mars's surface, thanks
to atmospheric blur and other factors.

face temperature than just the amount of sunlight reaching the planet. Because the Martian atmosphere is very thin, much of the Sun's heat is not trapped, as it is on Earth. Instead, it reradiates, or bounces back into space. A hot day on Mars is about −4 degrees Fahrenheit and a really cold day drops to a shattering −133 degrees.

FEAR AND TERROR

One of the ironies of science is that scientists have often come up with correct ideas based on unsound reasoning. Such was the case when Johannes Kepler turned his attention away from the orbit of Mars to the possibility that satellites might be orbiting the planet. He figured that because the Earth had one moon and Jupiter had four, the Red Planet, orbiting in between, should have two. By chance, Mars does have two moons, but not because of any neat mathematical "fit." In Kepler's day, only four of Jupiter's moons were known. We know today from the *Voyager* missions that there are at least 16 moons circling the giant planet!

Though "predicted" by Kepler in the seventeenth century, the two Martian moons Phobos and Deimos, names meaning "fear" and "terror," were not actually found until 1877. Finding them was not easy because the moons are very small and irregular in shape. They have been compared to giant potatoes. Phobos is only 16 miles long and Deimos 9.3 miles long.

Phobos is a speed demon and whips around the planet in just under eight hours. Deimos takes

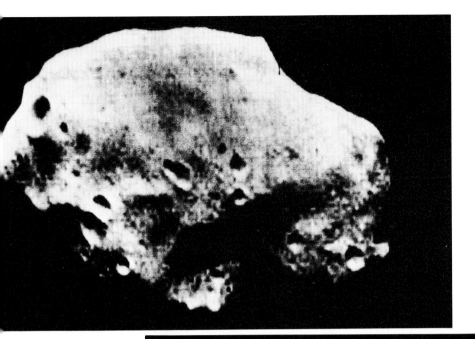

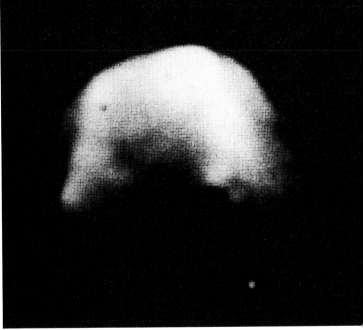

Mars's moons
Phobos (top) and
Deimos, as seen
by *Mariner 9*.

just a few hours longer to circle the planet than Mars takes to rotate once on its axis. This makes the two moons appear to move in opposite directions. If you were sitting on the Martian equator, Phobos would streak across the night sky in only four hours. Deimos, on the other hand, would take sixty hours to cross in the opposite direction. The apparent reverse orbit of Deimos is much like two automobiles traveling in the same direction along a highway. To the occupants of the faster car (Mars rotating), the slower car (Deimos) appears to be going in the opposite direction.

Up to the middle 1960s, all information about Mars was obtained by observing the planet with the naked eye or using a telescope when the planet was closest to Earth, about 35 million miles away. However, even with very large telescopes, 35 million miles is still a great distance. Much better observations could be taken at close range.

CHAPTER THREE
EARLY
MARS VOYAGES

In the middle of the 1960s an invasion began. It was not a Martian conquest of Earth as told by science fiction writers but that of Earth spacecraft invading Mars. Their intent was entirely peaceful. They probed the planet to learn its secrets.

The first attempt to fly to Mars was made with a NASA robot spacecraft called *Mariner 3*. The mission lifted off on November 5, 1964, and immediately ran into trouble. A shroud or shell covering the spacecraft during launch failed to come off in space, as it was supposed to, trapping the spacecraft inside. With the cover still in place, none of *Mariner 3*'s instruments would work, and many months later, the spacecraft passed Mars, missing the planet by a wide margin.

The failure of *Mariner 3*, though disappointing, was not surprising. After all, the space program was still in its infancy. The first successful Earth satellite, the Soviet Union's *Sputnik 1,* had reached space just seven years earlier, and *Mariner 3's* mission was much more ambitious. Rather than just climbing to an orbit a few hundred miles above Earth, *Mariner 3* had to travel more than 130 million miles to reach Mars. The great distance from the Earth to Mars was partly due to the fact that Mars doesn't stand still in orbit. The spacecraft had to be aimed along a complex trajectory toward the place in space where Mars would be more than 200 days later. Just an error in speed of one mile per hour would make *Mariner* miss its mark by 9,000 miles!

A second spacecraft, *Mariner 4,* was ready to follow *Mariner 3* a few days later, but because of the shroud trouble, engineers delayed the launch until a new kind of shroud could be built. *Mariner 4* took off for Mars on November 28, 1964. Except for the usual "bugs" that still plague even the advanced space probes of today, *Mariner 4* was wonderfully successful. The 575-pound spacecraft, consisting of 138,000 pieces, looked a bit like the blade portion of a windmill. From the middle of the spacecraft's body, with its instruments, radio, and control systems, extended four large rectangular solar panels, covered with solar cells to make electricity. The panels had to be large because the intensity of sunlight on Mars is less than half of that received on Earth.

Mariner 4 carried eight scientific instruments. Most of the instruments sought to learn about the planet's radiation and magnetic field. The most exciting instrument was a television camera that would take the first close-up pictures of Mars. Today we are used to seeing wonderfully detailed color pictures of the outer planets made by the *Voyager* spacecraft. By comparison, the *Mariner 4* pictures of Mars, taken during its brief encounter with the planet as it shot by at a distance of only 6,118 miles, are very crude. Yet even with the primitive technology in use then, the pictures were nearly fifty times better than could be made from Earth.

A total of 21½ pictures of Mars were taken, one every 48 seconds, and recorded on 300 feet of computer tape. Each picture, consisting of 250,000 bits of computer data, took eight hours of radio time to transmit, at a rate of 8.3 bits per second. (The *Voyager 1* spacecraft, when it flew by Jupiter fifteen years later, was able to transmit more than 115,000 bits per second.) The first of the pictures was taken at a distance of 10,500 miles away and showed an area slightly above the Martian equator in the region named Elysium Planitia. The pictures revealed relatively flat terrain occasionally pockmarked with craters.

The next *Mariner* spacecraft was sent on to the planet Venus, but *Mariners 6* and *7,* launched in February and March of 1969, continued the Martian odyssey. Each was a 900-pound version

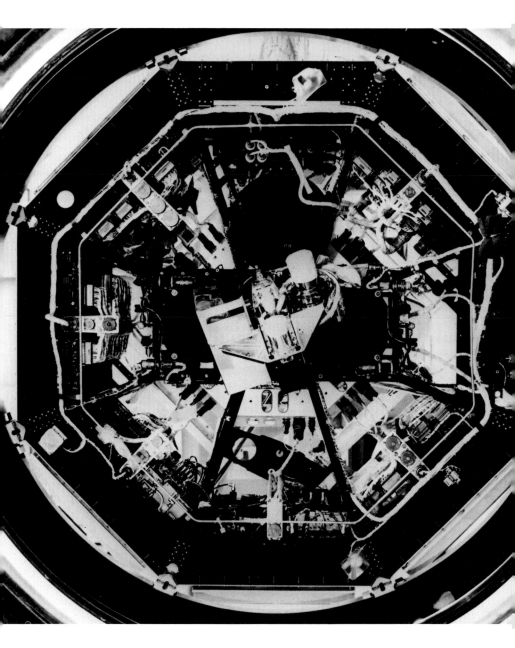

The television camera (center) used by *Mariner 4* to take the first-ever closeup pictures of the planet.

of the earlier *Mariner 4* spacecraft with greatly expanded scientific instrumentation for studying the Martian atmosphere and greatly improved data-transmission capabilities. The normal data-transmission rate for the two advanced *Mariners* was 270 bits per second, a thirty-two-fold increase over *Mariner 4*, and a high bit rate of 16,200 per second for special applications.

The purpose of *Mariner 6* and *7* was to evaluate surface conditions on Mars and gather evidence as to whether those conditions would be conducive to some form of Martian life. They were not to determine if life actually existed there. That determination was to be made by missions planned for the next decade.

Mariner 6 and *7* also featured greatly improved television systems. A single picture was composed of 3.9 million bits of data as opposed to the 250,000 in a *Mariner 4* picture, resulting in much sharper and more detailed images. During their closest encounters with the planet, objects on the surface as small as 900 feet across could be seen, an improvement of 600 times over the best pictures taken with Earth-based telescopes!

As with *Mariner 4*, the pictures from *Mariner 6* and *7* showed relatively flat terrain speckled with shallow craters. Other areas were more heavily cratered, with many craters 30 to 50 miles in diameter. The spacecraft also found bumpy "chaotic" areas of low ridges and small valleys, plus rills similar to the meandering trenches found on the Moon. Measurements of the Martian atmosphere pointed to very thin air with temperatures ranging from −189 degrees F at the south polar cap to 62 degrees F during the day in the equatorial zone.

To some scientists studying these data from Mars, the results were somewhat disappointing. Though only about 20 percent of the entire Martian surface had been photographed close up, what was seen indicated that the prospects for life were poor. If life forms did exist, they would have to be very primitive to survive the harsh conditions on Mars.

One scientist in charge of the television studies of Mars went so far as to state that future astronauts landing on the planet for the first time would "find a rather uninteresting terrain for the most part." Considering that all the pictures of Mars sent back by *Mariner 4, 6,* and *7* revealed similar features, this scientist's conclusion is easy to understand. However, sweeping statements such as this are always dangerous to make. Mars still held many secrets, and the planet was anything but "uninteresting"!

THE NEW FACE OF MARS

According to an old saying, anything that can go wrong will go wrong. Such was the case with *Mariner*s 8 and 9 in 1971. But what started out in disaster ended up as one of the great planetary missions of all time.

*Mariner*s 8 and 9 were designed as orbital spacecraft that would fly to Mars and circle the planet, taking thousands of pictures and atmospheric, temperature, and surface composition measurements. *Mariner 8* took off for Mars first, on May 8, 1971. The launch vehicle was a two-stage rocket consisting of an Atlas first stage, famous for its use in propelling John Glenn into space to become the first American to orbit the Earth, and a Centaur upper stage. The Centaur was a cryogenic rocket, meaning that it used supercold liquid hydrogen and oxygen for its propellants. During liftoff, the Atlas performed well, but the Centaur stage failed to ignite properly, dooming the mission to failure.

The *Mariner 9* spacecraft being mated to the Atlas Centaur launch vehicle.

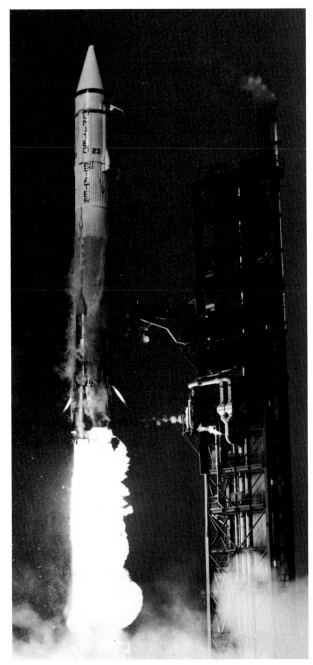

Mariner 9 is launched from Cape Kennedy in Florida at 6:23 p.m., EDT, May 30, 1971. At that time, Mars was 63 million miles from Earth.

The next try at the planet came just twenty-two days later, and this time both rocket stages worked perfectly. *Mariner 9* was on its way to Mars. All was going exceptionally well when a new problem arose, not a problem with the spacecraft but a problem with Mars. Two months before the spacecraft was due to orbit the planet, a dust storm started in the Hellespontus and Noachis regions of the Martian southern hemisphere. Regional dust storms are common on Mars, but this storm began to spread until the entire planet was shrouded in dust. Astronomers had never seen a storm so extensive on Mars or one as long-lived. When *Mariner 9* fired its braking rockets on November 9 to enter orbit, the storm was still in its fury and showed no signs of abating.

The swirling dust was so dense that *Mariner 9*'s camera system could only make out a few features on the planet—the south polar cap and four darkish spots. With no opportunity to take pictures of Mars, scientists decided to make the best of the situation and direct the two television cameras of the 974-pound spacecraft toward the Martian moons Phobos and Deimos. The cameras produced the first ever close-up views of the two moons and revealed them to be irregular in shape and pockmarked with craters.

By the end of 1971, the planet-wide dust storm began to subside. Gradually, like layers of curtains being drawn aside, the surface of Mars opened for inspection. Scientists who had lamented that Mars was a "rather uninteresting place" joyfully "ate" their words. Mars was filled with magnificent sights that rivaled the imaginary Martian features created in books by Edgar Rice Burroughs sixty years before. Rather than a "dead" world of broad plains sculpted with meteorite craters billions of years ago, as seen in *Mariner 4, 6,* and *7* photographs, Mars was revealed to be a dynamic world of stunning landforms.

The four dark spots turned out to be massive volcanoes. The largest of the four, Nix Olympica, was already familiar to astronomers. However, they had mistakenly believed that the circular feature they occasionally saw through their telescopes was a giant meteorite crater. Rather than a circular depression, it was shown by *Mariner 9*'s television photography to be a volcanic mountain almost three times taller than Mount Everest on Earth. The mountain was later renamed Olympus Mons (Mount Olympus). At its base, the volcano is 335 miles in diameter— almost big enough to cover the state of Ohio. The caldera, or crater at its top, is large enough to drop the state of Rhode Island inside.

Though the results of past volcanic activity— volcanic cones, large lava flows, and dome-shaped parcels of land pushed upward by the pressure of the molten rock beneath—were identified at nineteen different sites on Mars, signs of current volcanic activity were not observed by *Mariner 9*. This fact was not surprising. Active volcanoes on Earth can lie dormant for hundreds of years between eruptions.

This global mosaic of Mars, based on 1,500 computer-
corrected TV pictures of Mars taken by *Mariner 9*
in 1971 and 1972, shows the north pole's ice cap
(at the top), along with exciting landforms.

The great Martian mountain named Nix Olympus,
soon after to be renamed Olympus Mons, was
shown by *Mariner 9* to be almost three times
taller than Mt. Everest on Earth.

More startling than Olympus Mons was the discovery of a rift or crack renting the crust of Mars. The rift dwarfs the Grand Canyon on Earth. Starting to the east of the four volcanoes mentioned earlier, the rift, named Valles Marineris, stretches more than 2,500 miles. A similar canyon on Earth would reach across the United States from San Francisco to Washington, D.C. In some places, the sloping drop from the canyon rim to the floor is more than 20,000 feet. If you could stand at the rim, you would have difficulty seeing its opposite side, which can be as much as 150 miles away.

Mariner 9 was the spacecraft that made the tantalizing discovery of many small riverlike channels on Mars that were much too tiny to be seen with telescopes on Earth. Their discovery led to the obvious question of what force caused them. The channels were too meandering to have been produced by cracks in the planet's crust, and there were no signs of volcanic activity nearby that could have produced channels with lava flows. The channels had every appearance of having been cut by running water. For example, they showed signs of braiding, a common water-erosion feature on Earth, and many tributaries. If water did cut the channels, where was it now? The land appeared desert-dry.

Observations of the Martian polar regions pointed to one possible answer to the missing-water question. Because Mars, like Earth, has a tilted axis, its hemispheres alternate between winter and summer. As the Martian north polar

Mariner 9
reveals a great
rift, the Valles
Marineris, in
Mars's crust.
The Grand
Canyon on
Earth is tiny
in comparison.

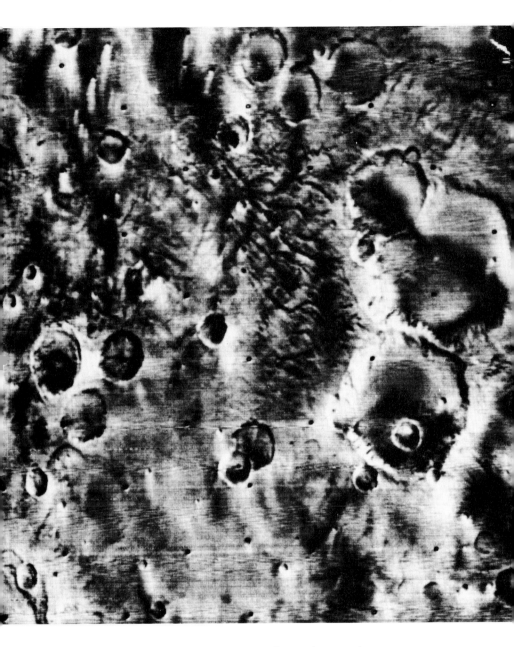

Small, riverlike channels can be seen here
among the numerous Martian craters.

cap grows, the southern polar cap recedes and vice versa. Because the Martian atmosphere is predominantly carbon dioxide gas, it was easy to determine the nature of the polar cap ice. When carbon dioxide gas drops below −109 degrees F, a temperature easily reached in the Martian polar regions during winter, it freezes out as dry ice. During the polar summer, as the temperature climbs above −109 degrees F, the dry ice evaporates back into gas. However, the diminishing of the northern cap in summer only goes so far and then stops, even when the temperature rises well above the freezing point of carbon dioxide. There is a whitish residue left behind. Scientists think the residue is not dry ice but water ice. Polar temperatures normally do not reach 32 degrees F, which would permit water ice to melt and flow out across the Martian surface as rivers.

Mariner 9 data led scientists to speculate that the Martian north pole has a small permanent ice cap of water ice perhaps several miles thick. Sometime in the Martian past, volcanic activity or very long-lasting dust storms, trapping the Sun's heat, could have temporarily warmed the planet, triggering melting of the permanent caps and initiating flooding that produced some of the river channels. Later, as the planet chilled down again, the water condensed out in the frigid polar regions to re-form the permanent caps. Other channels, however, seem to have been formed by water welling up from beneath the soil.

The strong probability that water existed on Mars in quantity reinforced scientists' hopes that Mars might harbor life forms. It was time to send spacecraft probes to the Martian surface.

CHAPTER FOUR
THE VIKING
SPACECRAFT

Even while *Mariner 9* was still orbiting Mars, NASA was already hard at work on a new Mars-exploring spacecraft. The next step to Mars would be a big one—a landing on the Martian surface. The mission was named *Viking*.

Landing on another world, though a very difficult feat, was not impossible. NASA had accomplished this several times with the robot *Surveyor* spacecraft that had landed on the Moon and with the *Apollo* Moon-landing missions. Landing on Mars, however, would be a much bigger feat. When the *Apollo* astronauts landed on the Moon, they had the advantage of being able to make on-the-spot decisions and to alter their landing plans quickly to fit unexpected situations. *Apollo 11* commander Neil Armstrong had to steer his lander away from a boulder field on the Moon before he and Edwin (Buzz) Aldrin could touch down. However, the *Viking* lander would not be under human control. If it were to come down over big rocks that could cause it to crash, *Viking* could not hover while a radio "Help!" message was sent to Earth for new instructions. The round trip for the radio messages alone would take at least thirty-five or forty minutes, and fuel would be exhausted long before help could arrive! *Viking* would have to make its own landing decisions.

As in several previous NASA missions, there would be two *Viking* mission spacecraft. This strategy had proven successful on a number of occasions. If one *Viking* spacecraft failed, the other one could complete the job.

As scientists put in their requests for the experiments they would like *Viking* to carry, it became apparent that each of the two *Viking* spacecraft should consist of two parts—an orbiter and a lander. It also became apparent that the *Viking*s would have to be much larger than the *Mariner* spacecraft that preceded them to Mars. The spacecraft would weigh more, require more propellants to slow them down for orbital insertion, need larger solar panels, require more data-handling capabilities, and take at least twice as long to get to Mars.

THE VIKING ORBITER The 5,125-pound *Viking* orbiter would serve as the "bus" to carry the *Viking* lander into Martian orbit and as the scientific data communications relay. Its basic structure would consist of an octagon approximately 8 feet across. Elec-

An artist's representation of the *Viking* orbiter, with
the lander underneath in its protective "aeroshell."

tronic equipment would be mounted behind each flat face of the structure. From the octagon would extend four windmill-like solar arrays that would increase the diameter of the entire spacecraft to 32 feet. Covering the 161 square feet of surface area of the four arrays would be thousands of solar cells to make electricity from sunlight.

Communications with Earth and the lander on Mars were to be accomplished by using three separate radio antennas. One antenna would be a steerable high-gain two-way antenna for communications directly with Earth. To work, it had to point directly at Earth. It could receive instructions from Earth and send back data at a rate of up to 16,000 bits per second. A second low-gain omnidirectional (meaning "in all directions") antenna could be used for communications when *Viking* was still near Earth and could also be used in an emergency to reestablish radio contact with Earth if the high-gain antenna lost its fix on Earth. However, because omnidirectional antennas send their signals in all directions, these signals, thus spread out, become very weak. The third antenna would be designed to receive radio messages from the lander craft on Mars, to be relayed to Earth using the high-gain antenna. The reason for doing this would be efficiency. The lander would have an antenna for communicating directly with Earth, but because Mars rotates, the planet itself would block communications with the lander for approximately twelve hours each day. The orbiter, placed in an orbit that would keep it over the lander and in communication with it at all times, would be blocked by the planet for only a few hours each day and therefore could communicate with Earth for longer periods without being interrupted.

Guidance and control of the orbiter as it traveled to Mars would be accomplished by two tracking sensors. One would sense the position of the Sun and the other would lock on to the position of the star Canopus. As long as the Sun and Canopus were in their proper places, the orbiter would be angled in the correct direction. If one or both stars were not in their proper places, this would mean that the orbiter had rotated from its correct position and adjustment would be needed. Navigation with *Viking* would be very similar to the way people on Earth navigate by the stars. (For example, if you want to walk north at night, just keep the North Star directly ahead of you.) If correction became necessary, small nitrogen gas jets, located at the tips of the solar arrays, would fire, producing rocket thrust that would re-aim the spacecraft.

During Mars orbital insertion (MOI), the guidance system would become especially important. Even a slight error could cause *Viking* to miss the planet entirely or plunge into the atmosphere and burn up. When proper alignment was achieved for MOI, a large rocket engine, mounted on the opposite side of the octagonal structure from the lander, would fire to create a braking thrust, permitting Mars's gravity to capture the spacecraft and put it into orbit.

The *Viking* orbiter would carry its own suite of scientific instruments. Essential to the selection of a safe landing site would be a pair of 1,500mm focal-length-lens television cameras. Both cameras would be specially designed to scan potential landing sites and later do detailed mapping of the entire surface of Mars.

A second instrument on the orbiter would be an atmospheric water vapor detector. *Mariner 9*'s studies of Mars pointed to the existence of water on Mars, but scientists could not determine if Mars was locked in an ice age or if its water supply was evaporating into space. The water vapor detector would be a spectroscope, which breaks light into its component "colors" so that their wavelengths can be measured. Water vapor in the atmosphere filters out certain wavelengths of light, and the detector would be designed to respond to those wavelengths.

Finally, an infrared mapping device would be installed to measure temperatures on the Martian surface, at the polar caps, and in the clouds. By operating over the planet for many months, the infrared device would provide important information about seasonal changes on Mars.

One additional experiment would be possible with the orbiter. Although its radios would not be designed as scientific instruments, there would be times when they could provide valuable data. Twice during each orbit, radio signals from the orbiter would pass through the planet's atmosphere on their way to Earth. Distortions in the radio signals would provide information about the density of the Martian atmosphere.

THE VIKING
LANDER The *Viking* lander would be a much more complicated affair than the robot *Surveyor* spacecraft that landed on the Moon in the mid-1960s. Unlike *Surveyor,* the *Viking* lander would have to pass through an atmosphere before landing. In addition, prior to loading on the launch vehicle, the entire lander would have to be carefully sterilized to destroy any Earth microorganisms planning to hitch a ride to Mars.

The lander spacecraft would consist of five basic systems. The first would be the lander itself. It would be a hexagonal box with three long sides and three short sides, giving it a triangular appearance with the three corners snipped off. The box would be constructed of aluminum and titanium metal alloys and would provide support for scientific experiments, communications equipment, and landing rocket engines. Three folding legs would extend from the short sides. When extended, the legs would hold the box 8.7 inches above the ground. At the end of each leg would be 12-inch circular footpads.

The second basic system of the lander would be its *bioshell.* After all the lander parts were sterilized, they would be assembled and encased in a two-piece white shell looking somewhat like a slightly flattened egg. The *Viking* egg, however, would be 22 feet in diameter and 6.4 feet thick. It would act to prevent Earth microorga-

Artist's drawing of the
Viking **lander on Mars.**

In this artist's rendering of events happening on Mars, the *Viking* lander, still in its aeroshell, is being lowered by parachute onto the Martian surface.

nisms from "nesting" in the lander. For its flight to Mars, the bioshell, with the lander inside, would be attached to the orbiter spacecraft opposite the rocket system that would be used to slow the two-part spacecraft for MOI.

Prior to the actual landing attempt, the lower half of the bioshell would be discarded and an inner shell, a third basic lander system, called an *aeroshell,* would protect the lander during entry into the atmosphere of Mars. Though Mars's atmosphere is very thin compared to Earth's, the speed of the lander's entry would generate enough friction to burn up many lander systems. The aeroshell would consist of a flat cone of aluminum alloy covered with a corklike material. During intense heating, the cork would burn off, carrying away the heat while leaving the inside relatively cool.

The fourth basic lander system would be a *cover* and a *parachute* that would mount to the top of the lander on the opposite side from the aeroshell. At the right moment during landing, the cover would be ejected and a parachute 53 feet in diameter would shoot out to slow the lander much like parachutes are used on Earth to slow drag racers.

The remaining basic system would really be a cluster of devices to aid in the landing. The actual touchdown on Mars would not be achieved by parachute because the parachute could accidentally settle down on top of the lander, covering up its cameras or causing the lander to be dragged across the Martian surface should strong ground winds be encountered. The landing would be accomplished by a set of three rocket engines. Each engine, burning hydrazine propellant, would have 600 pounds (2,600 newtons) of thrust, which would be more than enough to lower the 1,270-pound lander to the surface. In the low Martian gravity, the lander would actually weigh only 483 pounds. The nozzles of the three engines would be of a unique design. Each engine would actually have eighteen small nozzles to spread out the thrust in order to protect the Martian surface from the blast and avoid causing injury to any possible inhabitants.

Other parts of the landing systems would include communications equipment to communicate with the orbiter and with Earth, radar devices to calculate accurately the elevation of the lander as it came down, a guidance and control system, computer data-storage systems, and an electrical power supply. The power supply would consist of two 35-watt radioisotope thermal generators. Each generator would convert the heat produced by the radioactive decay of plutonium into electricity. Waste heat would be used for keeping the lander systems warm during the cold Martian nights.

All of the basic lander systems would really have one purpose—to determine what the Martian environment was like and see if it was suitable for life. Most of the instruments carried by the lander would be very complex. Included would be a television station that would permit pictures of the Martian landscape to be taken, including 3-D pictures; a small weather station for measuring temperature, pressure, and wind speed; automatic chemical laboratories for conducting complex chemical and biological tests; an arm and a scoop for digging up Martian soil; a miniature conveyor system for transporting the samples to the onboard laboratories; a magnetic particle detector; and a seismometer for measuring Marsquakes. The same amount of equipment on Earth, which would normally fill several buildings, would be miniaturized to fit inside

Liftoff!

a shallow three-legged work station a mere 10 feet across!

LIFTOFF In the late afternoon of August 20, 1975, the powerful Titan III Centaur rocket, holding the *Viking 1* orbiter and lander in its expanded shroud, stood on its Florida launch pad. At 5:22 P.M., Eastern Daylight Time, the powerful engines of the Titan first stage came to life. A thunderous roar swept across the nearby Florida landscape. Slowly at first and then gaining speed, the mighty rocket propelled *Viking 1* on its way to Mars. It was a flawless launch. Less than three weeks later, on September 9, 1975, the scene was repeated with *Viking 2*.

CHAPTER FIVE
THE
NEW MARS

By mid-February, *Viking 1* had passed the mid-point of its trip to Mars. It had traveled over 89 million miles and had approached to within 15 million miles of Mars. *Viking 2* was following behind at a distance of 3 million miles. By the end of March, with only eighty-five days remaining in its voyage, *Viking 1* had reached a velocity of 61,000 miles per hour (mph) relative to Earth and 5,500 mph relative to Mars. (The different relative velocities of *Viking 1* were due to the different speeds and orbits of the Earth and Mars.) The spacecraft played a game of catch-up with Mars, coming at the planet from behind as both planet and spacecraft traveled in nearly the same path and direction around the Sun.

With few exceptions, the voyage of the two *Viking*s went smoothly. *Viking 2* had battery-charging problems, but ground controllers radioed new instructions to the spacecraft that corrected the problem. By May 1, still a month and a half from the planet, *Viking 1* sent its first picture of Mars back to Earth. Still at a distance of 7 million miles, the image of the planet was about one-third the size of the Moon as seen with the unaided eye from Earth. Not much detail was present, but a slight fringe at the southern polar cap was evident. Mars's gravity was beginning to have its effect on *Viking 1*. By June 19, 1976, the day of MOI, the spacecraft's velocity had increased to 8,000 mph. The rocket engine on the orbiter fired for thirty-eight minutes to slow *Viking* and put it into Martian orbit.

Two days after *Viking 1* arrived at Mars, a brief firing of *Viking*'s engines trimmed the orbit slightly. This put the orbiter's cameras at a favorable altitude to examine the landing site selected from *Mariner 9* photographs of Mars taken five years earlier. The orbit chosen was a large egg-shaped one that would carry the orbiter high over the planet when taking large, wide-angle pictures and close up when taking more detailed shots.

A short while after *Viking* went into orbit, scientists and engineers on Earth decided that the primary landing site was too rough. What had seemed level and smooth in the *Mariner 9* pictures turned out, in the better-quality *Viking* orbiter pictures, to be crisscrossed with gullies and craters and littered with large boulders. The discovery that the chosen landing site was unsuitable was a great disappointment to many, because they had hoped the actual landing would take place on July 4, 1976—the two-hundredth anniversary of the United States. Landing a spacecraft on another world would have been a wonderful way to celebrate. However, since a crash landing seemed likely, it was better to wait until a more suitable spot could be located.

On July 20, 1976, another anniversary of importance—that of the first *Apollo* Moon landing, seven years earlier—the *Viking 1* lander began its descent to the Martian surface. The great egglike shell protecting the lander separated from the orbiter, never to return. From then on the two spacecraft, which had traveled 440 million miles through space together, would remain connected only by radio links. Seven minutes later, small liquid-fuel rocket engines in the lander's heat shield fired for 22 minutes and 16 seconds to break its orbit and begin the long arcing fall to the surface. The spot chosen was the Chryse Planitia region, a broad and smooth basin on Mars north of its equator.

On Earth, engineers and scientists anxiously waited in the control room at the NASA Jet Propulsion Laboratory in Pasadena, California, watching dizzying displays of flashing lights and television screens as the computers responded to radio signals received by huge radio dish antennas spaced around the Earth. They watched with excitement and with great frustration. Even traveling at the speed of light, the radio signals took nineteen minutes to reach Earth. That meant that what they were seeing was something that happened nineteen minutes in the past. If troubles arose during the landing, there was nothing they could do about it because it had already happened and was over.

As expected, the heat shield, on going through the Martian atmosphere, began experiencing friction. Though thin, the atmosphere heated the outside of the shield, burning off the corklike cover. Had there been Martians to watch on the surface, the event would have looked like the flaming streak made by a large meteor falling from the sky. Sensors on board sniffed the air so that scientists could determine its composition. Just four minutes after first encountering the atmosphere, the lander reached an altitude of 19,273 feet above the planet. The mortarlike cannon pushed the red-and-white parachute out to billow in the air, and the lander quickly slowed from 519 to 118 mph. A few seconds later, explosive bolts severed the connection to the heat shield, and it tumbled away to crash on the surface. The three lander legs stretched out for the first time in hundreds of days and locked into position.

The last sixty seconds of the descent to the surface were left to be handled by the three clustered nozzle rocket engines near the lander's base, as the parachute was jettisoned and slowly fluttered to the surface some distance away. *Viking 1* touched down on Mars at 8:12 A.M., Eastern Daylight Time. Nineteen minutes later and 220 million miles away, jubilant engineers and scientists began cheering. Their revelry soon turned to awe when the big television screen began displaying the first picture of Mars taken from its surface. The *Viking* cameras scanned the surface a small swath at a time, and the black-and-white picture on the display back on Earth was built up the same way. Gradually, rocks appeared, and between the rocks was dusty soil. The Sun was off to the right, causing medium-sized shadows to extend off to the left. Soon, the circular footpad and part of one landing leg appeared. Later, the cameras were directed off to the horizon, which appeared to be about 2 miles away. The "smooth, safe" *Viking 1* landing site was littered with rocks of all sizes. One rock 10 feet in diameter, big enough to flip over the lander if it had come down on top of it, lay only 25 feet away. The rock was later nicknamed "Big Joe." Small sand dunes, in addition to the rocks, could be seen in the distance.

Meanwhile, back in space, *Viking 2* was making its approach. It followed *Viking 1* into orbit on August 7 and to the surface on September 3, 1976, in the Utopia Planitia region, 4,000 miles west of the *Viking 1* site. *Viking 2*'s trip to the surface was especially tense for the waiting scientists on Earth. Just seven minutes after separation of the lander from the orbiter, nearly all radio contact with it was lost. A power failure had reduced the radio link to just a small flow of data. Fortunately, the *Viking* lander was able to automatically switch to a backup system. Landing instructions had already been sent to the spacecraft's computer, and it knew exactly what to do. Full communications with the lander were

In this early picture of the Martian terrain near *Viking 1*'s landing place, many rocks can be seen. "Big Joe" is on the extreme left.

not reestablished until after the landing. Its first two pictures of the Martian surface were lost, but the third was soon received. Again, the supposedly smooth, safe landing site was a rock- and boulder-strewn plain. Both *Viking* landers were now at work on Mars while their companion orbiters circled the planet from above.

SURFACE INVESTIGATION BEGINS

Immediately upon landing, *Viking 1* told scientists that the surface of Mars was strong enough to support a heavy spacecraft. Upon direction from Earth, its scanning cameras peered all around the landing site. Most of the pictures *Viking 1* took and later those taken by *Viking 2* were black and white, but special filters on the cameras were used occasionally to generate color pictures. As one would expect on the "Red Planet," the fine dust and sandy soil of Mars were rusty red. The rocks, however, ranged from

various shades of gray to slightly red. As pictures from both landers became available to scientists, comparisons revealed that the two landing sites resembled each other, but there were also differences. Both sites looked very much like the deserts of the southwestern United States, but without the cactus and Joshua trees. The Utopia plains were more rolling than the land at the *Viking 1* site. The *Viking 1* lander at the Chryse site observed a greater variety of rock types, while at Utopia the rocks appeared to be mostly of a bubbly volcanic type. Rocks at Chryse seemed to have wind-polished faces, and nearby were small, rippled sand dunes. In some places bedrock, not loose rock on the surface but rock solidly attached to the planet, was visible. No sand dunes or bedrock was observed at Utopia, but shallow troughs in the surface were seen crisscrossing nearby.

Above: this is one of the first color pictures
to be sent back to Earth from Mars, proving
the "Red Planet" was indeed red. *Facing:*
sand dunes in the Chryse Planitia Basin.

Eight days after its arrival, *Viking 1* extended its robot arm to collect its first soil sample. The arm was a 10-foot-long tube that unrolled from a small motor-powered reel near the lander top. The tube was an ingenious device consisting of two pieces of flexible metal; it looked somewhat like a wide version of the metal used for steel tape measures. While rolled up on the drum, the metal pieces were flat, but when they were extended, they each popped and curled along their lengths to form two halves of a rigid tube. At the end of the arm was a jawlike device for digging trenches and scooping up soil samples for the chemical laboratories on the landers. The arms were so strong that they could even be used to push over small boulders to sample the soil beneath. The soil beneath rocks on Earth is often full of small living creatures, and it was thought that rocks on Mars just might host similar living communities.

MARTIAN WEATHER FORECAST Studies of the Martian atmosphere and weather were an essential part of the *Viking* mission, and from the moment each lander set down, it began serving as a weather station. A small weather station boom, or arm, extended upward to sample the Martian winds. Fixed to its end were a temperature sensor, a pressure sensor, and a device for determining wind speed and direction. Day after Martian day, rather dull Martian weather forecasts were sent to Earth: "Light winds coming in from the east by late afternoon, changing to the southwest after midnight. Wind speeds will range up to 15 miles per hour. Low temperatures will plunge to below minus 122 degrees Fahrenheit, and the high temperature will climb to minus 22 degrees in midafternoon. Barometric pressure 7.70 millibars [about 1/125 the air pressure on Earth].''

Perhaps the greatest surprise about Mars's atmosphere was the color of its sky. Scientists assumed that Mars would have a blue sky, just like Earth. The lander cameras, which took pictures of the sky, showed it to be pink to orange instead. Scientists attributed this to the presence of reddish Martian dust in the air. Though the sizes of the dust particles were probably very small, about 1/125,000 of an inch across, there was so much of it suspended in the air by Martian winds that it changed the air's color.

In spite of differences in color and pressure, scientists were also surprised to learn of the many similarities of the Martian atmosphere to Earth's. The daily temperature of both planets peaks at about 3:00 P.M. local time. The day-to-night temperature ranges at both lander sites are similar to the temperature ranges in deserts on Earth, though Mars is colder. Winds over the Martian plains seem to follow the same patterns as winds on the Great Plains in the United States. Both planets have clouds and fog. Though the Martian atmosphere contains only about 1/1,000 as much water as Earth's, the water condenses out as ground fog in small Martian valleys during the night to evaporate during the day. The *Viking* orbiters observed high clouds forming and swirling about the summits of the Martian volcanoes. One big difference, however, was a long-

Sunset, computer-enhanced style,
over the Chryse Planitia region.

term drop in the atmospheric pressure on Mars as the Martian winter approached in the southern hemisphere. Scientists theorized that carbon dioxide, the primary gas in the Martian atmosphere, was freezing into dry ice at the south pole and lowering the atmospheric pressure over the whole planet as a result. At the lander sites themselves, a coating of frost would form each winter. Scientists believe that carbon dioxide condensed out as dry ice around dust particles in the atmosphere and settled to the ground as "snow."

From the atmospheric-sniffing experiments conducted as each *Viking* lander descended to the Martian surface, scientists learned that 95 percent of the Mars air is carbon dioxide. The remainder is mostly nitrogen (2.7 percent) and lesser amounts of oxygen, argon, and a variety of trace gases. The discovery of a small amount of nitrogen was exciting to scientists because nitrogen is an essential part of living things on Earth. Because of the low Martian gravity, as compared to Earth's, it was not surprising that so little nitrogen was present. Much of the gas that was present when the planet formed probably escaped long ago into space. Scientists speculated that if there had been much more nitrogen present in the past, there might also have been much more water in the atmosphere. Combining these factors with a temperature range that was not too cold for life led scientists to say that the prospects for finding life on Mars had increased greatly.

The soil sampler scoops up some Martian dirt, to be sent to the *Viking* onboard laboratories.

THE SEARCH FOR LIFE

Viking 1 stood on the Martian surface for eight days before the search for life began in earnest. Scientists had hoped that the lander's cameras might have picked up signs of life, such as nearby plants or footprints, but none were ever seen. The question of life would now be up to the complex miniature science laboratories hidden in the lander's interior. Gradually, the sample arm rolled out, shoved the scoop at its end into the ground about 6 feet away, and grabbed some soil. Carefully, the soil was brought back and poured into a funnel where it was sieved to eliminate pebbles. Then the soil was divided among the laboratories. But not all the soil entered the laboratories. Small magnets, mounted on the scoop, collected magnetic soil particles.

From what was left behind, scientists estimated that about 5 percent of the soil was a mineral similar to the mineral magnetite found on Earth. Analysis of part of the soil sample in the chemical laboratory indicated that it contained 42 percent oxygen, 21 percent silicon, and 13 percent aluminum, with the remaining 24 percent comprised of magnesium, calcium, sulfur, chlorine, titanium, and potassium. The rest of the soil was sent on to the biology laboratories.

Three small biology laboratories served as incubators for "hatching" Martian life. Long before *Viking* was launched, scientists determined it would be impossible to carry enough equipment on board *Viking* to detect every kind of life that might be present. Instead, they made two assumptions. The first was that if life existed on Mars, it would be carbon-based, like that on Earth. Second, if life were common on Mars, the Martian soil was likely to be saturated with microorganisms that could be detected with various chemical tests.

Three life experiments were sent to Mars on *Viking*. The first would check to see if carbon dioxide was being taken in and converted into organic (carbon-based) compounds. On Earth, plants do this. The second experiment would check to see if certain gases were being given off, as they are by organisms on Earth. Finally, a special radioactive "food" solution was fed to a third sample to see if radioactive carbon dioxide gas was expelled. If so, that gas could be detected.

At first, scientists were elated at the results that were being transmitted to Earth. In each experiment, something was going on that could be interpreted as the action of living things. The results were tantalizing, but scientists stopped short of concluding they had found life on Mars. While they pondered, tabloids at supermarket checkout stands on Earth shouted at shoppers with "Life on Mars!" headlines. Scientists groaned when they saw the headlines. They knew that hasty conclusions often lead to later embarrassment. More data were needed before they would confirm that there was life on Mars. Furthermore, the chemical analysis experiment failed to detect any organic compounds (carbon-based chemicals that make up living things). They couldn't understand why lifelike reactions were taking place when no other signs of organisms, living or dead, could be detected. In their own laboratories on Earth, biochemists and other scientists tried to repeat the same experiments that were going on in the *Viking* landers. Eventually they achieved similar results with nonliving materials. This left open the distinct possibility that what was taking place on Mars were exotic chemical reactions that only mimicked life. The question "Is there life on Mars?" was left unanswered.

MEANWHILE, BACK IN SPACE   As each *Viking* lander probed the Martian surface and searched for life, the orbiters overhead continued their scans of the surface. They continued to provide daily high-resolution pictures of a far better quality than those sent to Earth five years earlier by *Mariner 9*. They looked at the huge volcanoes, craters, great canyons, and the mazes of twisting, water-cut channels. At one point, the *Viking 2* orbiter was instructed to change orbits to enable it to fly over the Martian polar caps. Its pictures and measurements confirmed earlier *Mariner 9* pictures that pointed to a perennial core of water ice at the polar caps. In warmer times that water ice would have been liquid, and it would have flowed over and carved out channels on the planet. Also found sticking out from under the northern polar cap were many thick horizontal layers of what might have once been windblown dust. If so, these layers would contain historical records of the Martian climate.

Mars from space seems like a divided planet. Most of the land in the northern hemisphere is at a lower elevation than the land in the southern hemisphere. The north is mainly windblown dusty plains that change appearance during the Martian seasons, while the south is mostly crater-covered but with craters that are different from those on Earth's Moon. After impacts from meteorites, the Martian soil flowed in rivers fanning out from the crater, indicating that there had once been ice beneath the crater which had been melted by the heat of the impact. Most of the planet's great volcanoes are arranged along three parallel lines in the northern hemisphere. Because of their immense size compared to volcanoes on Earth, scientists speculate that the crust

Valles Marineris, the Grand Canyon of Mars.

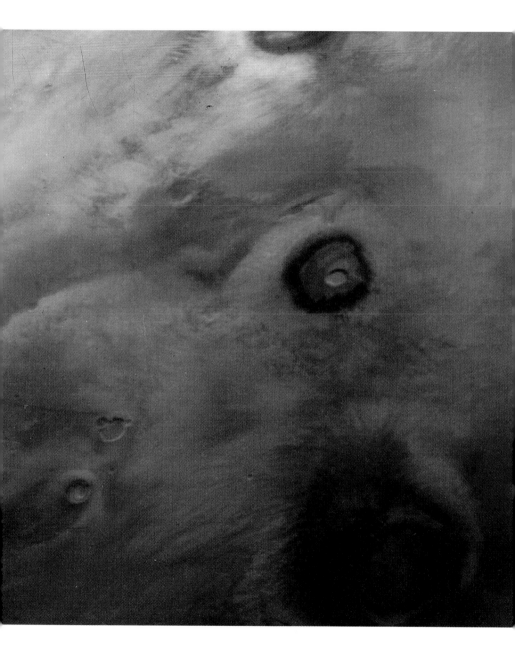

Tharsis Ridge is the major volcanic province of Mars.
Three volcanoes on the ridge can be seen in this picture.

Top: this dazzling
artist's rendition
of Olympus Mons
reveals a volcano
that would just fit
inside the borders
of the state of New
Mexico. *Right:* this
false-color photo
of Olympus Mons
shows variations
in lava flows over
a period of time.

of Mars must be much thicker and more stable than the Earth's crust. With little crustal movement, eons worth of volcanic eruptions have piled up in the same place to form huge mountains that only a thick crust could support. The crust of Mars is thought to be 150 miles thick, and the planet's core is between 800 and 1,300 miles in diameter.

Like *Mariner 9,* the *Viking* orbiters also took close-up looks at the Martian moons Phobos and Deimos. The pictures were so clear that craters just a few feet across could be seen on the surface of Phobos. Scientists speculated that Phobos was an asteroid that had been captured by Mars's gravity long ago.

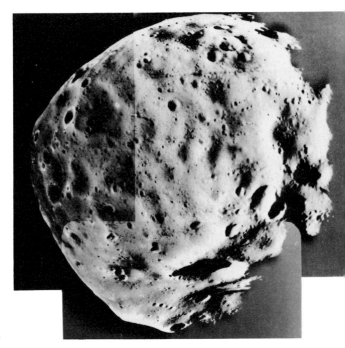

Phobos as seen by *Viking 1.*

CHAPTER SIX
THE VOYAGES
CONTINUE

The late Thomas A. Mutch, a NASA scientist and administrator, summed up scientists' feelings about the success of the *Viking* missions: "Eight years of planning, moments of frustration, friendships forged by common problems, and now everything happening just as we had disbelievingly promised each other it would." It was hard to believe that four robot spacecraft millions of miles away, resting on and circling an alien world, could work so well and accomplish so much.

The *Viking* landers were only supposed to last a few months on Mars, but those who had built them saw to it that the spacecraft were built very well. The *Viking 2* orbiter finally ran out of attitude-control fuel on July 25, 1978. Without thrusts from its attitude-control system, it could no longer point itself in the right direction to continue its surveillance of the planet. The last message to Earth from the *Viking 2* lander was received on April 11, 1980, and then it fell silent. The *Viking 1* orbiter also ran out of fuel in the late summer of 1980. The *Viking 1* lander continued stubbornly working on Mars until November 1982, when it suddenly fell silent. Engineers continued sending radio commands in an attempt to reestablish communications, but the lander failed to respond. By the following May, all efforts were discontinued, and the *Viking* mission was terminated.

"Terminated" is a harsh word, but it applied only to the data-gathering phase of the program. Still going on even today is the main reason the *Vikings* were sent to Mars in the first place—the analysis of the data the four spacecraft sent back. *Viking* has given scientists a cornucopia of scientific data they will ponder for years to come. Scientists, true to form, are not totally satisfied and want much more data. Left unresolved are many important questions, not the least of which is the question of life on Mars.

NASA began formulating plans for follow-up missions, including *Viking*-like landers but with tracked (tanklike) wheels so that the landers could move about on the surface. What if there were life on Mars, but it was just over the hill where the stationary *Viking* landers could not see? More advanced roving landers, looking something like the Lunar Rover used by astronauts on the Moon, were also envisioned. Still other plans envisioned scooping up samples of Martian soil and loading these samples aboard a small rocket that would use the lander as a launch pad. Back in

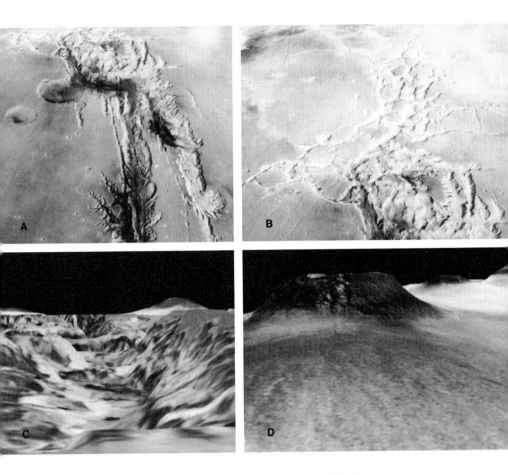

Work on *Viking* data continues to this day.
This recently released series of photographs
shows four computer-enhanced images of Mars,
created by scientists at the Jet Propulsion
Laboratory in Pasadena, California. (A) is
the surface of the western portion of Valles
Marineris; (B) is the Labyrinthus Noctis,
an intricate system of canyons; (C) is a view
from the edge of Ophir Chasma, the northern
part of Valles Marineris, looking across the
canyon; and (D) is a view of a series of giant
volcanoes in the region of the Tharsis Montes.
In the foreground is Arsia Mons.

orbit, the rocket would be captured by an orbiting spacecraft that would, in turn, send it back to Earth's orbit in a larger return vehicle. There, waiting scientists on a space station would analyze the Martian materials. The most ambitious plans of all were those that envisioned sending astronauts to Mars for direct exploration. NASA had originally hoped to have manned expeditions to the Red Planet before the end of the 1980s, but budget problems and changing national priorities put these plans temporarily aside.

Halfway around the world, the Soviet Union launched its own ambitious mission to Mars in 1988. The Soviets sent twin spacecraft named *Phobos 1* and *2* to orbit Mars and study the Martian moon Phobos from very close range. This was not the first time they had attempted to go to Mars. In the early 1970s, they made three landing attempts on Mars. Though they reached the planet, two of the spacecraft crashed and a third stopped working after twenty seconds. The Soviets hoped the *Phobos* spacecraft would break their string of bad luck, Unfortunately, a ground controller sent commands containing an error to *Phobos 1,* causing the spacecraft to lose contact with Earth. *Phobos 2* reached Martian orbit, but its communications lock with Earth was lost while gathering data. However, the failure was not total, because *Phobos 2* did relay some valuable information about the space environment of Mars, and some pictures of Phobos were taken to compare with pictures taken by the *Viking* orbiters.

The Russians sent their space probe,
Phobos, to Mars in 1988.

This artist's drawing of a future Mars mission
shows a transportation depot in Mars orbit and
the extraction of resources from Mars's moons.

Mars is now back high on NASA's planning list, with a late 1992 or 1993 launch of the *Mars Observer* spacecraft. Rather than attempting a landing on the planet, this spacecraft will spend a Martian year in orbit directing a suite of eight instruments, including close-up and wide-angle cameras. It will scan the planet for surface composition, atmospheric, and magnetic field data. It will measure the planet's gravitational field, the altitude of surface features, and try to learn more about the role water has played in shaping the surface of Mars. Information sent back by the spacecraft could provide the data needed for humankind's next big step into space.

On July 20, 1989, the U.S. president, the vice president, the administrator of NASA, the astronauts of the *Apollo 11* mission, and many other dignitaries joined for a celebration of the twentieth anniversary of the first human step on another world. They assembled on the steps of the National Air and Space Museum in Washington, D.C. Just inside the doors were displays of the actual aircraft used by Wilbur and Orville Wright in their famous first flight, the *Apollo 11* command module, and a *Viking* lander. President George Bush, after congratulating all those who were involved in the historic first manned Moon landing, pointed the U.S. space program back at the Moon, saying that the time has come for us to return to stay. The time has also come, he said, to begin planning an even bigger step— human exploration of Mars.

GLOSSARY

Aeroshell. A cone-shaped shell that protected the *Viking* landers as they entered the atmosphere of Mars.

Bioshell. A cover around the *Viking* lander spacecraft to keep out Earth organisms that might hitch a ride to Mars.

Chryse Planitia. The general location of the *Viking 1* lander on Mars.

Deimos. One of Mars's two tiny moons.

Inner planets. The four planets of the Solar System closest to the Sun: Mercury, Venus, Earth, and Mars.

Mariner 4. The first successful spacecraft to fly past Mars and transmit pictures of its surface back to Earth.

Mariner 6. Advanced version of the *Mariner 4* spacecraft that flew past Mars.

Mariner 7. Advanced version of the *Mariner 4* spacecraft that flew past Mars.

Mariner 9. A Mars-orbiting spacecraft that transmitted to the Earth thousands of pictures covering nearly the entire surface of Mars.

Mars Observer. A proposed new U.S. space mission to the planet Mars.

Mars Orbital Insertion (MOI). The firing of retrorockets (braking rockets) to slow the spacecraft so that they could be captured by Mars's gravity and begin orbiting.

Martian canals. Nonexistent features once thought to crisscross the surface of Mars.

Phobos. One of Mars's two tiny moons.

Phobos 1 and 2. Ill-fated Soviet spacecraft to Mars.

Utopia Planitia. The general location of the *Viking 2* lander on Mars.

Viking lander. The portion of the *Viking* mission spacecraft that landed on the surface of Mars.

Viking orbiter. The portion of the *Viking* mission spacecraft that remained in Martian orbit.

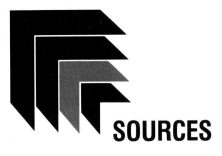

SOURCES

Ezell, Edward Clinton, and Linda Neuman. *On Mars: Exploration of the Red Planet, 1958–1978.* NASA SP–4212. Scientific and Technical Information Office, 1984.

NASA Jet Propulsion Laboratory. *The Many Faces of Mars.* JPL Technical Memorandum 33–654, 1973.

NASA. *Mariner Mars 1971 Press Kit.* NASA Headquarters, 1971.

NASA. *Mars: The Viking Discoveries,* NASA EP–146. U. S. Government Printing Office, 1977.

NASA. *The Martian Landscape.* NASA SP–425. Scientific and Technical Information Office, 1978.

NASA. *Viking Encounter Press Kit.* NASA Headquarters, 1976.

NASA. *Viking Orbiter Views of Mars.* NASA SP–441. Scientific and Technical Information Office, 1980.

NASA. *Viking: The Exploration of Mars.* NASA EP–208. U. S. Government Printing Office, 1984.

Weaver, Kenneth F. *Journey to Mars.* National Geographic Society reprint, 1973.

FOR FURTHER
READING

The National Aeronautics and Space Administration has published many interesting and beautiful books on the Viking mission and what was learned about Mars. Here are a few:

Mars: The Viking Discoveries. NASA EP–146. U.S. Government Printing Office, 1977. A readable and not too technical look at the *Viking* discoveries about Mars.

The Martian Landscape. NASA SP–425. Scientific and Technical Information Office, 1978. Technical but filled with excellent pictures and descriptions of the surface of Mars.

Viking Orbiter Views of Mars. NASA SP–441. Scientific and Technical Information Office, 1980. Technical but filled with excellent pictures and descriptions of Mars as seen from orbit.

Viking: The Exploration of Mars. NASA EP–208. U.S. Government Printing Office, 1984. A general book about Mars and the Viking mission that contains many beautiful pictures.

INDEX

Moon-landing missions, 59

National Aeronautics and Space
Administration (NASA), 41, 59, 60,
75, 96, 98, 101
Newton, Sir Isaac, 33, *34*

Olympus Mons (Nix Olympica), 50,
52, 53, 93
Ophir Chasma, *97*
Orbit(s)
of Earth, 11, 35
elliptical, 21, 31, 32
of Mars, 11, 31, 35
planetary, 21, 31, 32
Outer planets, 31, 43

Phobos, 38, *39,* 40, 49, *94,* 98, 104.
See also Moon(s).
Phobos spacecrafts, 98, *99,* 104
Planets
apparent motion of, 20, 21
gravitational pull of, 33
orbits of, 21, 31, 32
physical properties of, 33
velocity of, 32

Red Planet, 11, 14, 18, 21, 35, 38,
78, *80,* 98

Satellites, 38, 42.
See also Moon(s).
Schiaparelli, Giovanni Virginio, 25,
26, 27, 29
Soil, Martian, 56, 69, 77, 82, *87,* 88,
90, 96, 98
Soviet Union space missions, 42, 98,
99
Spacecrafts, 15, 21, 29, 42, 57, 59,
60, 62, 65, 95, 98, *99,* 101

Spacecrafts *(continued)*
navigation and control of, 63
Sputnik 1, 42
Sunlight, intensity of, 36, 38, 42
Surveyor, 59, 65

Telescopes, 14, 21, 25, 29, *37,* 40, 45
Telescopic observation, 21, 33, 40
atmospheric effects on, 35, *37*
Television, 43, *44,* 45, 46, 49, 64,
69, 74-78, 87
Tharsis Montes, *97*
Tharsis Ridge, *92*
Titan III Centaur rocket, 71
Transportation depot, *100*

Valles Marineris, *54, 91, 97*
compared with Grand Canyon, 53
Venus, 12, 31
Mariner mission to, 43
Viking landers, 11, 60-63, 65-71, *66,*
67, 75-79, 83, 89, 95, 96, 104
onboard laboratories, 69, 82, *87,*
88
systems of, *61,* 65, 67, 68, 69,
75, 103
Viking missions, 12, 59-96
experiments and instruments on,
60, 64, 65, 69, 86
problems on, 73
Viking orbiters, 11, 60-64, *61,* 71, 74,
77, 90, *94*-96, 104
Volcanic activity, 50, 53, *94*
Volcanoes, 50, 83, 90, *92, 93*
Voyager missions, 38, 43

War of the Worlds, 13-*16,* 18-20
Wells, H. G., 14, *16,* 18, 19, 27

Year, Martian, 32

ABOUT THE
AUTHOR

Gregory Vogt, born in Milwaukee, Wisconsin, holds a bachelor of science degree (with a major in general science) and a master of science degree (with a major in earth science) from the University of Wisconsin at Milwaukee, and a doctorate in education from Oklahoma State University. He currently works for Oklahoma State University as an educational specialist on assignment to NASA's Flight Crew Operations Directorate at the Johnson Space Center in Houston, Texas, in the astronaut training division. In Oklahoma, Mr. Vogt was an adjunct assistant professor as well as the creator of special curriculum materials and computer software for NASA. He was also heavily involved in teacher training. Mr. Vogt was formerly executive director of the Discovery World Museum of Science, Economics and Technology in Milwaukee, Wisconsin. He has also been a writer/editor for Educational Publications at NASA headquarters in Washington, D.C., and an eighth-grade science teacher.

Mr. Vogt is married to Margaret Brunner Vogt, currently pursuing a master's degree in psychology. The couple has three daughters plus three pets—an Australian shepherd, a Dutch rabbit, and a guinea pig.